financial literacy for kids and young adults

Benjamin Amoah

Author: Benjamin Amoah

Copyright@ 2021 by Key Points Education, New York, NY

All rights reserved. Subject to the US Copyright Act of 1976. No part of this publication may be reproduced, distributed, or transmitted in any form or stored by any means, electronic, photocopying, or otherwise in a database or retrieval system without the author's prior written permission.

The author and publisher do not guarantee the completeness or accuracy of the contents of this book. They disclaim any warranties claimed to be implied or explicit.

Produced by Key Points Education, New York, NY

ISBN: 9798370300073
Imprint: Independently published

Acknowledgments

This book is dedicated to my family. Thank you for your phenomenal support.

Contents

Planning for your financial future	*1*
Budgeting	*7*
Managing your savings	*13*
Investing	*19*
Buying a home	*25*
Creating a business	*33*
Dealing in the stock market	*41*
Retirement funds	*47*

Introduction

You've probably heard the question, "When will I ever use that?" Kids at school say that about differentiating and integrating algebraic expressions or learning the symbols for elements on the periodic table. There are dozens of topics like this in curriculums taught in middle and high schools across the country. We wonder why students aren't taught topics that they will use.

Sadly, if you want to be successful beyond what most people can accomplish, you have to do the extra work and go after the knowledge you need to set yourself apart. Becoming financially literate is one of those important skills that virtually everyone needs in life. Without it, you're not set up to succeed very well when it comes to your finances. And finances have a huge impact on how your life turns out.

Just like basic Math and Communication or English literacy, becoming literate in finance is crucial. The impact of your finances on you and others in your life is why you should become financially literate. Now to be financially literate what do you need to know? Here is a quick list.

1. What does all the financial jargon like stocks, 401ks, and mortgages mean?
2. How to manage your finances at each stage of your life with budgeting, savings, and investments
3. What are the well-tested ways people make money today from their 9 to 5 jobs, buying stocks, starting businesses, etc?

4. And finally, how to maintain and grow your finances

You need to know these things to be set up for financial success. And the earlier you start the better.

Even though this book contains a rich amount of very useful financial advice, I do have to make the disclaimer that I am not a financial advisor, and the concepts, lessons, and topics discussed in this book are aggregated financial advice from financially successful people.

Chapter 1

Planning for your financial future

When it comes to managing your finances, there isn't one way of doing it. It all depends on your goals. You have to first think about what you want to see in the future. How do you want your life to turn out?

At an early age, it's hard to know what you want to do with your life. Because of this, it's also hard to know what type of financial future you want for yourself.

But the thing about setting goals is it doesn't always have to be so detailed. You can start with something very general and then as time goes on what you want becomes clearer to you. And so, the details don't matter right now. Just know that there's a better destination than where you are right now.

Let's start with a very general goal. The goal is that we want enough money. Maybe a bit more than just enough money so you can have some extra for things you don't know that you want just yet. That's a nice goal to start with.

So, you want some money. Where can you get some? Well, it first helps to know what money is. Money is used to represent value. And if you can create value, you can turn that value into money. As a society, we have agreed that money has as much value as any other thing we can create that has value in itself. Things that have value in themselves are things that people want. It is because people want them, that they have value.

If no one wants something, then that thing has no value to people. Money has value because people want it and people want it because as a society, we've agreed that money can be used to represent and store value.

Okay so now we know that to make money we have to make something of value. But as a kid, what value do I have to offer you might ask? Well, people would like to get tasks done within their businesses. As a young person, if you can get your parent's permission, you can apply for a job to help a business owner provide a service to their customers. You could work as a store associate at Walmart or McDonald's for instance. Waitressing is a common entry-level job.

So at least we know that we can offer some value in exchange for some money. But remember the initial goal that we set is to make enough money and not minimum wage. What can we provide that other people want so much that they are willing to pay a lot of money to get? Well, as a kid, there isn't much you can offer other than skills that a lot of people can provide and are willing to be paid minimum wage for.

The solution is to acquire skills that are scarcer in society. And not only skills that are scarce but these skills should be able to produce something that people want.

It could be something that is produced in low quantities but each unit has a very high value or it could be something produced in very high quantities in which case each unit does not have to have so much value.

Things that are produced in low quantities, but have a high value can be the service that you provide as a lawyer, surgeon, software engineer, or other jobs like this. With these examples, you exchange the limited number of hours and the skill that you have in a day in exchange for a high per-hour wage.

Things that are produced in high quantities, but have a low per-unit value are things like digital products like gaming apps, other kinds of software, and digital art, as well as physical products, like shirts, energy drinks, protein powders, and so on.

It's a good idea not to count any of these ways of making money. But the best advice that I've had so far about how to increase the value you can exchange for money is this. When you're earning power is very low, such as when you are still in school or immediately after you leave school and haven't saved up enough money yet, invest in yourself.

At this point in your financial journey, it is not the best use of your efforts to save every penny you make in the hope that you can build wealth that way. The amount of money you are making is too small at this point. It is best to invest in building yourself by acquiring valuable skills, and knowledge.

To get into a high-paying job as a lawyer, for example, you'll have to take the bar. This takes several years, but in the end, your skills can help you earn a high wage. Other high-paying jobs don't require so many years in school.

Software engineering requires you to show that you have the knowledge and ability to design and develop good software. You'll have to demonstrate the work that you've already done to convince a hiring manager, that you have the appropriate skill set for the job. The skills that they will be looking for will also include your ability to work with others because a lot of the time software engineering is a collaborative endeavor.

There are so many certifications out there in a broad range of specialist fields that you can study for and pass to make your résumé stand out.

Now, because there are only so many hours in a day that you can work, you'll realize that, even though you are making a high per-hour wage, you cannot save enough to make the amount of money you're looking for. This is where investments come in.

You have the option to buy stocks and bonds that will yield profits called dividends. You also have the option of saving up enough money to purchase a rental property. Typically, people do not save up enough money to buy the whole property. They only need a percentage as low as 5% of the value of the rental property and ensure that they have a source of income that will help them pay the rest to get a loan from a bank to buy that rental property. You'll have to pay the rest over some time, typically 15 to 30 years. This way you earn money by collecting rent.

You can also make your products which could be physical products like candy bars or digital products like an app on the Apple App Store.

With some of these options for making money, you will find that you don't have enough to invest. Sometimes you'll need to borrow money. You should be very cautious with taking on debt. Avoid it when you can. Especially bad debt.

Good debt is money you borrow to make a successful project like a business, even more successful. If you've found a magic formula that works for your business and you need more money quickly to take advantage of the growth, then you can leverage a loan.

Bad debt does not add value, it takes away value. An example of bad debt is expensive designer sneakers when you don't even have a coordinating top and pants to match.

Hopefully, you will make the right decisions about your decision to make money and to be cautious with debt.

One of my favorite sayings goes like this. "Everyone overestimates how much they can accomplish in a year, but underestimate how much they can accomplish in five years ". I repeat this quote in this book to emphasize it. What this means is that it's hard starting and there'll be many things to discourage you along the way.

Skills are really hard to learn in the beginning but once you've learned them well enough, it becomes very easy to repeat. This is why people are disappointed in what they can do in the beginning but are often very pleasantly surprised with what they're able to accomplish further on along the line.

You'll need to be creative and persistent, but if you continue to work hard, then you'll get to your goal. It might take you a long time or, who knows, maybe a short time. The important thing is to keep trying and learn from your many failures, and eventually, you'll have the finances that you want.

Summary:

1. How much money you can make depends on how much you can provide for what others want.
2. Don't save up pennies. Invest those in acquiring valuable skills.
3. There are high-paying jobs to help you save up enough money to buy investments like rental properties, stocks, and bonds, and start businesses.
4. Good debt helps you make more money, bad debt takes away money
5. Everyone overestimates what they can accomplish in a year but underestimates what they can accomplish in five.

Chapter 2

Budgeting

So much of life is determined by our habits. Because of this, it is so helpful to set up your surroundings in a way that promotes the behaviors that you want to adopt.

For example, if you want to increase the number of times you exercise in a week, it's a good idea to have exercise equipment in your room. If you want to eat healthier, you should make healthy food within reach and put all the chips and soda in a place that's hard to reach. Preferably let the snacks stay in the stores and not in your house.

Similarly, when you start to earn some money, you should create a budget and stick to it. Make it easy to stick to your budget by adopting behaviors that promote sticking to your goals. For example, if you want to save a certain amount of money each time you get paid, put money in your savings first, then put money towards your expenses. Why because it's easy to spend when there are so many ads online that tempt you to purchase all sorts of things you don't need.

Banks offer you products like checking and savings accounts. When you are old enough to open these accounts or you ask your parents to sign off on getting them, you can separate your money that way. Banks and other financial services companies have apps to manage your money. These apps typically have a feature where you can set up an automatic transfer to your savings account on the same day you get your paycheck. That way you can just act as if you get paid your paycheck minus your savings.

When your money is separated like this it's much easier to see your savings as untouchable until you're ready to use it for what you were saving it for.

Apart from developing good financial habits like saving, you should also remember to leave room to live life. What that means is many times, people who decide to save, either save too much or save too little.

Those who save too much put away so much of their money that they don't have enough left to experience life. You're saving too much money if you don't have enough left to afford adequate food or buy hygiene products to keep yourself clean.

Now if there are ways to save some money without negatively affecting your quality of life then go for it. For example, learning to cook is a valuable skill because it often costs much less money to cook than to get takeout all the time. You hone your cooking skills and save some money at the same time. You'll have to take into account the time you spend cooking and the cost of the food as well, and the gain of the enjoyment if you find out that you enjoy cooking.

Ok so let's say you've decided what you want to use your money for. You know how much should go to savings and how much should go to expenses. You may even have different things you want to save for. The key to budgeting is to not complicate it any more than you have to.

An example of a simple budget is this. You take out the portion for your savings. Then you divide the rest into the money for food, personal hygiene, and clothes. This is enough and not too complicated. Even simpler, you can divide it into savings and expenses. That's it. This makes your budget very manageable and freeing.

That way when you spend money meant for food on clothes, you know how to cut back or at least what you are sacrificing to afford clothes. This flexibility that simple budgets help you with less stress when managing your budget.

When budgeting, also think about your current goals in life and how your budget will help you get to them. If it's hard to think about your goals now, simplify the process like this. Where are you now and where can you go to get to and feel like you've gotten to a better place?

For example, would it be better if you knew more about finance, the stock market, programming, fashion, etc? Then save up to buy highly-rated online courses and books on these topics. Maybe study up for a certification on the topic you want. It would help you have an aim which would be the certification. Plus, you could include that in your resume when it comes time to apply for internships and full-time jobs. Would it be better if you had some gym equipment in your room? Maybe a couple of dumbbells and exercise bands. How about a creative studio? Your corner of creativity where you can practice your art, singing or writing, etc.

Now if you remain determined to always better yourself, eventually your earning power will grow. You will be able to afford more stuff. Avoid the temptation to spend more than you need to. Do you need the new iPhone with an extra camera that lets you see the pours in your skin in an even greater definition? Will that truly make your life better? Or could you spend a fraction of that on an experience with your family and friends and also have enough to pay for certification in an in-demand skill?

Eventually, all these skills you've learned when it comes to budgeting will be able to translate into other areas like budgeting for your business, side hustle, or house. Don't let your expenses exceed your earnings. And if you later on in life start borrowing money in the form of using a credit card or getting a mortgage, let it be to help you add to your wealth and not just for spending. In other words, borrow to buy assets and not liabilities. If you use a credit card to help you get the learning material for a difficult and rare certification like one in computer security, cloud engineering, or accounting, that's debt that gives you leverage to earn more than the amount in credit card debt you have.

Summary

1. Set up your life so the behaviors you want to encourage are easier to do.
2. Be responsible but don't cheap out on life experiences and miss your youth.
3. Simplify your budget. Don't make it too detailed so it's easier to keep track of it.
4. Your budget should reflect where you want to get to

Budgeting

Chapter 3

Managing your savings

Saving is putting aside resources so you don't experience a lack of those resources in the future. The first thing people think of when it comes to savings is money, but it can be much more than that.

The mindset to have when you're saving is you can earn far more making money than you can through saving money. Even people who earn high salaries that are significantly above average do not save enough to retire until many years into their careers. Remember that saving might not be the best bet to get rich or retire early.

Your focus should be to save but do not rely on it completely, especially early on in your career when the money you are earning isn't that much. Instead, focus on investing in your skills so you can get a higher-paying job and increase your earning power.

Kids and even some young adults don't realize how much they overestimate what working people make. A very good salary that's very much above average is $100,000 per year. If you earn this salary in say Florida or Texas where the cost of living and taxes are much less as compared to New York or California, then you're making an above-average salary.

If you do end up earning this much money, you still have to pay at least federal taxes to the US government and state taxes to your state depending on if they charge state taxes. But at least after federal taxes of about 18.5%, you are left with $79,500.

And then there are rent or mortgage payments, car payments, utilities, healthcare costs, food, clothing, and other expenses. Assuming after all these expenses you are left with $40,000, it would take you 25 years to save up $1 million. $1 million is a lot of money and you might receive pay raises along the way. But still, we are assuming that you will stay employed at this company for all those 25 years.

A job is not always guaranteed. It's important that apart from getting good at what you do in your day job, you should also work to create other sources of income outside of your main job. There's the possibility to make much more.

If we shouldn't rely completely on savings as a way to become rich, how should we think about saving?

Well, think of it as one of many ways to protect yourself and your loved ones financially. It is after all saving some of your resources now so that if you ever need it in the future, you will have something to fall back on.

You should develop healthy saving habits.

What are these habits? One is when you start earning some money, you should get into the habit of putting a portion of your savings aside first. If your money is in the same pool, you are likely to spend it as well. Separating your savings helps to separate it mentally as well and helps you pause to think if you indeed want to misuse it.

The second habit is developing your skill for determining cost. What I mean by this is for example, if you buy five cheap shirts that all fade within two months at $20 total, that's more expensive than buying only one quality shirt that could last you two years.

The third is to be healthy. Pay for a gym membership because it costs much less money and your quality of life than paying expensive medical bills and feeling tired with body aches at an early age. There's such a thing as "skinny fat". Even if you don't look overweight, it could well be that you're still unhealthy. So, take care of yourself. It'll save you a lot more than just money.

The fourth is learning to save dollars, not pennies. A lot of people are so focused on saving almost everything they make that they won't even invest in themselves. Instead of buying a book to improve their knowledge of a skill they are developing, they'll save that believing that's the best use for that money.

Get into the habit of saving to invest. To become skilled enough to earn 50 X the cost of the book each week is the wiser decision.

Four is building your emergency fund. This is also called a rainy-day fund. The typical advice is to save enough money to be able to live on for 3 to 6 months, but it should be as much as you are comfortable with. Maybe you want some buffer and so you want enough for 9 or more months. That's also a very good goal to have.

An emergency fund is not money you are saving to buy anything in particular. It is for critical circumstances that may come up. To help you with this, setting up an automated transfer to your emergency fund savings account becomes very helpful.

The fifth habit is getting back on track as quickly as possible when you deviate from your savings path. When you've spent money from your savings on something it was meant for, it is tempting to continue spending it on other things that it was not meant for.

For example, if you take money from your emergency fund, it's tempting to see other things that are just helpful or simply useful as emergencies. Save up for those other things. Don't prevent your emergency fund from recovering.

Finally, number six is to look at savings as something to maintain your growth. It should be a source of investment. However, improving your earning power is how you accelerate your growth and get wealthy. Many people think of saving as a way to get rich. But work to save to invest, while having an emergency fund as well of course. Invest so your savings can increase.

To put it simply, save to invest, and invest to grow your earning power.

Apart from the habits, you should develop around savings, it's important to know that where you keep your money also matters. You will probably be saving your money in a bank savings account. And especially for your emergency fund where you are likely to be saving for a while, choosing a bank that offers a high-interest savings account is a good idea. Make sure that they pay at least 2% interest.

Summary

1. Put aside the money for your savings first
2. Have a rainy-day fund as soon as you can
3. Don't save what you should invest
4. Your savings are meant to help sustain you while you get back on track, but your investments in yourself are the source of more savings and wealth.

Managing your savings

Chapter 4

Investing

As you grow up, it's vital to have an investment mindset. Almost everything you do can be considered an investment. If you choose to study hard in school or not, you're investing. If you choose to spend your time, playing video games or reading books, these are all investments.

And so, in your actions, consider what you are investing in. Is it something that's going to be beneficial to you or others? Or are you wasting a precious resource that could've been used for something useful?

Apart from investments for financial gain, it's important to realize that about extremely valuable things other than improved finances. It's important to invest in your relationships. Value the relationships that you have with your family, and with the good friends you experience life with.

You should also invest in things that promote a healthy lifestyle. Invest in a gym membership for instance, and use it. Or at least walk places if you can. Stay active and make it a habit.

It's extremely important to be balanced in the things you consider important and make the appropriate investment in all of them.

Now when it comes to finances, there are many areas in which you can invest. You can invest in stocks and bonds. You can invest in real estate. You can invest in a business or company. You can invest in a career.

Stocks are portions of ownership in a company that you can buy in a market, called a stock exchange. With some stocks, when the company makes a profit, you are given a part of it. The part of the profits that is given because you own a part of the company is called a dividend. But dividends are not the only means of gaining from buying stocks.

If there's a high demand for the stocks of a company, its shares, which are the units in which the stock is measured, will go up in value. When the share price increases, it means that the value of your stocks has also increased. For example, if you buy 10 shares of Tesla stocks at $300 each and after one year, there's been so much demand for Tesla stock that the share price has increased from $300 to $400, then, even though you bought those 10 shares for $3000, these same shares are now worth $4000. This means that if you sold your 10 shares now, you would have made a profit of $1000.

Bonds on the other hand are issued by a company or a government to raise some money with a promise to pay interest to those who bought those bonds. Government bonds are pretty stable. And the interest on those bonds means that you are for the most part guaranteed to receive a return on your investment when you bought those bonds.

US treasury bonds are considered one of the most stable bonds to buy in the world. Although it is possible for any government, including the US government, to default on paying back interest on the bonds they have issued. People do worry that if the United States continues to borrow so much money by issuing bonds because of its high rate of spending, then at some point, it will not be able to afford the amount of interest it has to pay on the bonds it has issued. And if the US ever defaults, people will lose trust in buying US treasury bonds.

I do talk more about stocks in another chapter.

Real estate has to do with buildings for housing and commercial purposes. When people want to buy a real estate property either for personal use as a home, or for commercial purposes, such as offices, manufacturing plants, or rental units in the form of apartments or condos, they can attempt to get a loan from a lender. This lender could be a bank. And the loan that you get from the lender is called a mortgage. I speak a lot more about mortgages and how to get one in another chapter.

You can also invest in an idea for a product or service by starting a business and growing it. Apart from the product or service a very important part of having a successful business is your ability to market it well. You have to be very determined to make a business succeed.

You also have to be willing to invest what it takes in terms of money and time.

Many people also have a hard time even starting a business. They spend a lot of time doing research without attempting to create a prototype of the product or service they want to sell.

An indispensable part of making a business succeed is acting on the idea and not only thinking about it.

It's also important to have a skill that is readily valuable to already existing companies. A lot of people have made a significant amount of money and built up their net worth by simply providing a very valuable skill to a company as their day job. They decided to focus on a career and got rich doing it.

When you're investing, look for areas where you can create leverage for yourself. Leverage typically means borrowing money and using it in an investment that will produce enough returns to pay back what you borrowed with interest and keep the rest for yourself.

Using a credit card to purchase an online course and to pay for a certification that is in demand is an example. With that certification and an impressive project or two to demonstrate your ability to do a job, you could get hired by a company that pays you many times what you spent in a single pay cycle of two weeks than what you spent on that certification.

If you take out a mortgage to purchase a rental property to rent it out, you are leveraging the mortgage to collect a profit in the form of a portion of the rent while you use the rest of the rent to pay back the mortgage over time.

In your investments, it is very important to remain open-minded and creative with how you can use leverage to generate wealth. You have to be creative with investments.

When investing it is important to diversify. This means not putting all your hopes in a single place. It's important to attempt to invest in multiple areas. This could be in stocks, real estate, private business, a career working for a company, or some other area I haven't mentioned here.

It is extremely risky to have all your investments in a single place. If you have a career, starting a business on the side reduces your risk of not having something to fall back on if you ever lose your day job.

Your skills, businesses, careers, relationships, all these things take years to develop. And so, it is important to start investing in them now. Typically, it's very difficult in the beginning. In-demand skills are very hard to learn. It might take you many, many, tries. But the key is not to give up. Continue to push until you get very good at it.

This is the same with business. It is extremely difficult, especially at the beginning when no one knows you or your product.

It might be very difficult to land your first job in a high-paying industry. All these are very difficult in the beginning. It's important to remind yourself of quotes like the following.

"Everyone overestimates what they can accomplish in one year, but underestimate what they can accomplish in five years. "

Summary

1. Investment is what you put into a project with the hopes of making it successful.
2. Aim to create leverage where you can
3. Diversify your investments
4. Invest in more than just making money but in healthy relationships
5. Invest in your health
6. Index funds have proved to be the safest financial instrument for the past 70 years
7. Diversify across industries, not across companies
8. Start nurturing income streams now to get the yield in the future

Chapter 5

Buying a home

Owning a home is one of the hallmarks of the American dream. As you become an adult owning one or more may become an option for you. But the process of getting to own can be difficult to understand for even grown adults. So, let's try to simplify things. What do you need to know about the process of owning a home?

Well, to get a home you'll have to buy one with money. A lot of people want to sell their houses, and new houses are built every year. These people will sell their houses for what is called a listing price.

You may have the choice to negotiate by offering to pay a lower price. They may or may not accept or they may come back with something lower than the listing price but higher than what you were offering. No matter how it turns out, you still need to buy the house with money.

The problem is that the average home price in America is about $350,000. This is a lot of money that most people can't afford. So, what do they do? Well, they go to a lender like a bank to borrow the money to buy the house.

The money that they borrow is what's called a mortgage. It's money they'll have to pay back each month over years. It takes some people 10 years, others 15, and others 30 years to ultimately pay back the mortgage to the bank. For some people, it might take as little as 5 years or even less. It all depends on how much they borrowed and how much they pay back each month.

Why would any bank give them this money? Well, banks have to pay the salaries of their employees and also make a profit from the money lending business they do. Because of this they will give out the money and allow you to pay it back while charging you a percentage extra every month. And that extra, called interest, is how they make money.

The borrowed money you pay back is called the principal or premium and the extra you are required to add to it is called the interest.

So, let's back up. Let's say you looked through a real estate website and found a house you want to buy. What are the steps from seeing it to buying it?

Typically, there will be a contact alongside the listing. This would usually be a real estate agent responsible for selling this house. If you have at least 5% of the listing price to put up as a down payment, you may be able to get the house. You will see down payments of as much as 20%. And that's good because it means the money you end up borrowing to cover the remainder is less, which also means that you will be paying less in interest on the mortgage.

After finding some houses online that you like, you should reach out to a real estate agent to guide you through the rest of the process. You also need to get a pre-qualification by asking the lender you found to give you one. Getting a pre-qualification can be done before or after you get a real estate agent. Regardless, the lender will need some documentation from you. This would include your bank statements for the past few months, pay stubs from your job, tax returns, social security number, etc. Your real estate agent may even recommend a lender to you where you can get this pre-qualification done. And so, whether you want to contact a real estate agent before or after your pre-qualification is done, that's up to you.

The pre-qualification will give you an estimate of how much you can afford to borrow in a mortgage.

After you have your pre-qualification, hired your real estate agent, and have the houses you are interested in, next is to call the real estate agents of the homeowners or the homeowners themselves, if they don't have real estate agents, and arrange for a tour of each of their houses. A tour of a property is called a showing.

If you like a house after you toured it, you can go to the lender and ask about getting a mortgage. They will ask for a bunch of documents just like during the pre-qualification stage. If you are approved, you will then move on to the last stage called escrow. This will include things like appraising the house to find its market value.

Once they have all this information and it looks good to them, they'll make the money available to the home or property owners if and only if the ownership of the house is transferred to you. Because this transfer of money depends on the agreement you sign in the form of a contract at the beginning of the escrow stage, we describe the money as held in escrow. When money is in escrow, it means that it will only be transferred to the receiver of the money if the people involved do what they say they'll do in the agreement.

Once the deed to the house is signed over to you and the escrow has been closed where the former owners got their money and all other costs like closing costs and the real estate agent's fees have been paid, then the transaction is now complete. You now own your own home and a mortgage which you will have to pay off every month for several years.

Remember, you do not begin paying a mortgage until the second month after the escrow is closed. For example, if you closed escrow in April, your first mortgage payment is in June, not May.

To summaries, the stages of buying a house are,

1. Pre-qualification (sometimes called pre-approval) to see how much you can afford to borrow
2. Hiring your real estate agent to assist you through the process
3. Touring houses of interest
4. Making an offer to the homeowners
5. Asking your lender for a mortgage
6. Going through escrow
7. Getting the deed to the house, meaning you now own it

The interest payments you will be making in addition to the original amount you borrowed on your mortgage, are determined by your past financial behavior.

How do they know your past behavior? Well, banks and other financial institutions can lend you smaller amounts of money in the form of credit cards, which you can use for small purchases. Since it is well known that those who show that they are consistent in paying back their debts are also more likely to do the same in the future, it makes sense to assign their borrowing history a high credit score.

You should aim for a high credit score.

At this point, you may have some more questions. What's the benefit of owning your home if you're going to owe a bank the money you used to buy the house plus extra because of interest? Why not just rent?

In some cases, it's better to rent your house or apartment rather than buy it. It depends on what you're looking for. The downside with renting is you are paying your money to someone else, the landlord. But maybe that's fine with you because you don't want to stay in that property for any longer than agreed upon in the lease agreement you signed to rent it.

If your rental lease is a one-year lease for example, and you've lived in the property for let's say seven months, you'll have to pay a fee to end the lease early. Although, people do sign monthly leases too which means you can leave the property anytime once you've paid the rent you owe if you still owe any. It also means that the landlord may have the right to end the lease at any time.

With renting you have that flexibility. On the other hand, when you own a property and you're paying a mortgage on it, the money minus the interest that the bank gets to keep, of course, is going to you. You are not paying it to a landlord. This means that you can sell the property, pay off what you owe to the bank including the interest up until that point and keep the rest. Remember, for example, if you have a 30-year mortgage, and you are selling the property in the 10th year, you don't pay interest on the remaining 20 years. Although some banks have a penalty payment for ending the interest payments early written in the mortgage agreement.

One other thing to remember is that initially, the majority of the payments you make each month on your mortgage goes to paying off the interest and a much smaller portion goes to the premium. The greater portion of your mortgage payments goes to paying off your premiums only later on.

So, what can you start doing now to prepare to buy your own house? Well, when you start earning a paycheck, start building your credit score. Whenever you spend money, and it's recommended that it's on something that gives you leverage, pay it off. Don't miss a single payment. Also, try to keep your credit card spending no more than 30% of the total money on the cards.

After some years of doing this, your score will go up. Work on staying in the 700s, so that eventually you may even reach the 800s. A score of 850 is the highest.

Start saving up for the down payment on the house, but more than saving up, work towards earning more. There is a limit to what you can save with a set income, but no apparent ceiling to what you can earn.

Finally, you can take it further by owning multiple properties that bring you a monthly income from rent by starting from one down payment on a mortgage.

If you can get a mortgage on a house or apartment, rent it out and use the money from the rent to pay the monthly mortgage. There may even be some money leftover as profit for yourself. This way you can save up and make another down payment on another property like you did the first time and rent that one out as well. Repeat the process until you're making quite a bit of profit from your rental properties.

Taking it a step further, after you have your first property with your first mortgage, you can exchange your current mortgage for a new one. This way you have the option of taking out the money that's been paid on the house so far. You can then use that money to make a down payment for a second property.

Let's say you bought an apartment for $250,000 with a down payment of $25,000 and a mortgage of $225,000. If you've paid off $50,000 in the premiums with the rent payments you were getting from your tenants. You can go to your bank to replace your current mortgage with a new one in what's called a refinance.

They can give you up to 80% of the apartment's market value. In this case, since the market value is $250,000, they can give you $200,000.

Since your original mortgage was $225,000 and you've already paid off $50,000 with the rent you've collected, you only owe $175,000 on the current $225,000 mortgage. And so, you can pay this remaining $175,000 you still owe using the $200,000 from the refinance money, leaving you an extra $25,000 which you can use for whatever you want. You can use it to make a down payment on a new apartment and rent that out as well.

These are simplified numbers so always remember the other costs as well like the closing costs on your second apartment.

Summary

1. You don't need the full amount to buy a house or rental property. Get a mortgage.
2. Build your credit score so the interest rates you have to pay on a mortgage will be lower.
3. If you rent, your money goes to a landlord. If you buy a house or apartment, the money goes to you.
4. Refinancing is an important way wealth and income streams are grown in real estate.

Chapter 6

Creating a business

Thucydides once said the following at the funeral of Pericles. "The secret of happiness is freedom, and the secret of freedom is courage." A huge percentage of those who dream of creating a company from an idea, never start it. Even more, people start bits of it but end up too busy watching Netflix and YouTube videos and scrolling through Instagram. But some want to start their company and put in a lot of effort. It just turns out that most of their energies are spent doing endless research about what they want to do.

They'll buy many online video courses and watch some of them but never actually get their hands dirty. And so, it turns out that the first step to starting a business is starting it.

You have so many options. Even now at your age, you can choose a skill to learn like video editing, graphic design, web development, database administration, etc., and create a profile on UpWork or some other freelance work platform to start your journey in the gig economy.

That way, you have some real-world professional experiences to talk about in future job interviews while earning a little bit of money along the way. You don't have to become an expert in the skill to start offering your services.

If it's a physical product, set a deadline of say, by the end of this week, you want to make five very crude versions of your product and store them in the business area in your room. Finish that first before you set the second deadline for the next part which may be setting up your online store on Amazon. Meanwhile, as you do these things you start saving up for the money you will spend on marketing on Amazon and possibly other platforms. You need to include in the budget, getting your packaging designed and taking professional photos of your product. Presentation is a huge part of the success of your product.

The main point of all this is to start now. And set tight deadlines, one deadline at a time to challenge yourself, give you a sense of urgency, and make the process fun because you're not focusing so much on perfection in the beginning.

Acting is what's important. Making many bad versions of something is far more likely to help you create a very nice version than spending a lot of time trying to make something perfect. You limit yourself when you are so worried about getting it right the first time. You will very probably be bad at things you don't have a lot of experience working on. At the onset, you will likely be very bad at it.

Even if you're trying to be perfect, you will probably suck at it.

Your aim therefore should be to make many bad versions of your product. The final product might even not have everything to the perfect standard that you want to eventually get to. If you believe it's a useful product that enough people would find useful or simply want then go for it. You can make it better over time.

After learning to act on your business idea, the other thing you need to learn is marketing. We all question whether we would ever use many of the subjects we learn in school, but the important subjects are those where you learn to communicate. English, visual art, music, and other subjects that allow you to develop your ability to communicate and communicate persuasively are crucial to the success of your business. How you present ideas have a big impact on how people will receive them.

There are countless people with impressive talents to sing but haven't worked enough on communicating their brand as a singer needs to. They get discouraged by the first signs of rejection and never move past that. What they needed was to carry on and get good at communicating who they are, presenting their music in persuasive forms that compel people to it.

However your product turns out, the vibe it has, its personality, its theme music, and its anthem are where it's at if you want people to see it, love it, and want it. But just like developing the product itself, the brand you market takes a lot of trial and error. It is going to take you doing it, learning from it, and doing it again. Well-established companies have to do this as well. It's a part of what makes a successful product. You don't necessarily have an end date for when you work on marketing if you want your product to continue.

Now even though you should find creative ways to market continually, you don't want to waste money just marketing to anyone everywhere. You should want to narrow your product to a target group. Is your product mostly purchased by kids who like video games or by adults in their 40s and 50s looking to improve their fitness? When you're able to narrow down your target audience, you can increase what's called, your conversion rate. This is how many people actually show interest and then purchase your product.

Social media sites offer these demographic and other data in their ads insights about those who are showing interest in your product when you advertise on their platforms. Take advantage of these features to know your audience.

Because people are bombarded daily with so many products and services, you should try to keep your product very simple at first. It should preferably do one thing, maybe two, for your customers. It should be simple and beautiful. If it does a lot of other things, highlight the most compelling features in your ads.

A core principle of success in business creation is persistence. It's often the difference between those that make it and those that don't. Many businesses failed because they gave up too soon.

But building a business should also be a learning process. And at times when things aren't working, it's important to be able to step back and observe what moves the company closer to success and what is dragging it back. Are there any key obstacles that you can remove or get around or even better turn into something that moves it forward?

Stepping back means regrouping. And sometimes you may see a new path that will help the business succeed. Other times you may see that your product in its current form is not something enough people want.

Whatever the case may be see your business journey as a fun, challenging experience with so many options. Don't get stuck and obsessed with only one way of getting your business to succeed. Don't also fall for the sense that your product idea is so good that you can't come up with others that are as good. Don't even accept that you have to work on only one idea at a time.

It's a non-medical disease called one-itis. See options where they exist and don't limit yourself.

There's a TED talk by Bill Gross, titled "The single biggest reason why start-ups succeed" where he talks about research on the main factors that determine if a business will succeed or not. You can find it on YouTube. At the end of the talk, he reveals that timing was the most significant factor.

If you've noticed, blockbuster movies are released in the middle of summer or during the holidays. Horror movies come out during Halloween. Christmas-themed movies come out during the Christmas period. These are examples of timing releases for when they'll have the most success.

Other examples are alcohol commercials during the Super Bowl because that's when a lot of adult sports fans purchase huge quantities of alcohol. There are discount deals advertised during Black Friday, Cyber Monday, and throughout the Christmas shopping season.

The lesson from this is to learn to take advantage of timing. But more than that learn to ride the wave of trends. It's even much better if you can predict when a trend will start so you can be ready to take advantage of it. If there's a trend in a particular period and you happen to have a product that fits that trend, try to make use of the opportunity.

The final point is to spend what you need to spend to make the product successful. What you'll find is people can save up for expensive pieces of clothing, video game consoles, and expensive concert tickets, but feel like they're throwing money away when they spend money on marketing their product, buying ads on social media, getting professional photos of their products taken, etc.

You should communicate the quality of your product by working hard on the brand. Don't waste money by not listening to the feedback you get from customers and the data you see in your ad analytics that social media sites provide during your ad campaigns. But spend the money you need to spend.

Summary

1. Ideas are a dime a dozen. Working on the idea is what's important.

2. Do your research but don't only do research. Act. Don't overthink, don't overanalyze.
3. Marketing and communication are critical skills for a successful business.
4. Keep your product simple at the beginning, learn from customer feedback and then improve.
5. You will get several chances, not just one.
6. Timing is everything when launching a product.
7. Spend what you need on your business

Creating a business

Chapter 7

Dealing in the stock market

Some companies do very well, but to continue growing, they need to invest in the development of new products and improve on existing ones. To do this, they need to raise money. And so, they go to the stock market and allow the public to invest by buying shares. In other words, they make their companies public. What that means is they sell shares which are tiny bits of ownership of their companies to the public.

How do you participate in owning shares in a company? If you'd like to own a part of their company, you can go to the stock market and purchase some of their shares. As the company grows the demand for its shares also increases. And so, if you bought their shares at $10 per share, and the demand for their shares increased, because of how well they are doing, the share price may increase to let's say, $15 per share. What that means is if you decide to sell your shares now you would have made a five-dollar profit on each share. On the other hand, if the company doesn't do well after you bought the shares and the price goes down to four dollars per share then you would have lost six dollars on every share you bought.

So, there's a potential for gaining on the stock market or losing. But the key with the stock market is to not panic when your share price goes down. The price of shares on the stock market goes up and down all the time and it's up to you to determine when to buy and when to sell. The goal is to buy low and sell high. That is, you need to buy shares when the price per share is low and wait till the price is higher than you bought it before selling. The problem is it is extremely difficult to predict when a share price will increase or decrease.

Everyone who owns shares in a company is said to own stocks in that company. But not everyone owns an equal number of shares. The one who owns 10 shares owns stocks in a company and so does the one who owns 10 million shares.

Those who own a significant percentage of a company are described as having a stake in the company. They are called stakeholders.

Because the share price of a company can go up and down pretty quickly, it is wise to buy shares from many different companies so that you don't put all your eggs in one basket.

Fortunately, there's a way to buy shares in a bunch of companies without having to go find many individual companies to buy shares in. You can simply invest in something called a mutual fund. A mutual fund is a huge amount of money from many investors that have been used to buy shares in a lot of different companies. The different shares that were bought are called a portfolio. And some mutual funds have a diversified portfolio.

There are different types of mutual funds, but the one that most people end up investing in it's called an index fund. The S&P 500, for example, is a very popular index fund because it has shares in 500 of the most successful companies in the United States. These companies are from a very diverse set of industries. From tech to pharmaceuticals to retail, transportation to hospitality, and many more.

When it comes to index funds like the S&P 500, over the past 70 years, it's always trended upward. Over the past 70 years, it's grown in value at an average rate of 11% per year. That means that if anyone bought $100 of stock back then, it would have grown in value to $148,802 today.

And so, the key to being successful with your investment in the S&P 500 or other consistent index funds, is to be a passive trader. What that means is if you buy shares in the Vanguard S&P 500 index fund, you leave your investment untouched for many years. People who tend to trade the S&P 500, trying to buy low and sell high on a day-to-day basis end up losing money because it's hard to predict when prices will rise or fall.

You can trade stocks through brokerage firms, like Vanguard, TD Ameritrade, and Fidelity. You can buy shares on their platforms online or download their mobile apps. There are small fees for each trade you make.

There are also very popular apps, run by fin-tech companies, like Robinhood, SoFi, and others where you're able to buy fractions of shares. Although, increasingly the brokerage firms, I mentioned above offer fractional shares as well.

The stock market is a very emotional place to be. This is because you see your hard-earned money either go up or down. There's always the temptation to sell when the share price of your stock is going down. You'll be tempted to sell to stop further losses.

But typically for very well-established companies, the share price may go down for a day, a week, a month, or even an entire year during a recession. But they very often come back up. Shares in companies like Apple and Google tend to trend upward.

Remember that an index is just a calculation of a portfolio of stocks of different companies. To invest, you need to invest in an index fund. This is where money is used to purchase actual shares of different companies. For example, the S&P 500 is an index. But an example of an index fund that tracks the S&P 500 is the Shwab S&P 500 index fund.

In terms of indexes, the S&P 500 is not the only one. The others like the Dow Jones Industrial Average, NASDAQ Composite, and the S&P 100. They may have slightly different focuses for the industries that make up their portfolios.

It would be up to you to do your research to determine which funds to invest which portion of your long-term investments in.

Summary

1. The key to trading stocks in the stock market is buying shares at a lower price and selling at a higher price
2. Index funds are a type of mutual fund. A very popular index fund is the S&P 500
3. Apps that allow you to trade in the stock market are Robinhood, SoFi, and TD Ameritrade.
4. When the stock market goes down, it doesn't necessarily mean you've lost your money forever
5. Your safest bet is to buy shares in an index fund, particularly the S&P 500

Dealing in the stock market

Chapter 8

Retirement funds

One of the ways people prepare for the future is to save up some money so that when they are no longer working, they will still have a source of income to sustain themselves.

If you simply save money over decades, the value of your money will decrease because things tend to cost more year on year because of inflation.

Because of this, they put their money in a retirement fund called an IRA. This stands for Individual Retirement Account.

As the name implies, this is a fund that you pay into yourself. There are providers of this service online. On the other hand, there is a 401k. This is the retirement account that your employer creates for you.

With a 401k, you decide the percentage of your salary you want to go into it. Some employers will match your contribution. What that means is, they'll put into your 401k the amount you put in up to a certain amount. Some people will choose to put in the maximum at which their employer will match them. They don't want to leave any money on the table.

If you decide to have an IRA, you would have the choice between a traditional IRA and a Roth IRA. The difference between the two is when you pay taxes on your contributions to the retirement fund.

With a traditional IRA, you don't pay any taxes on your contributions now, you only pay later on when you're ready to take your money out.

The Roth IRA has taxes now but no taxes when you are taking your money out.

For both types of IRA, you pay a penalty if you take money out before you turn 59 and a half years old. Although with the Roth IRA, you won't pay any taxes or penalties if you use the money to buy a home for the first time or to pay for college.

You are limited on how much you are allowed to put into your 401k. The limit is a little over $20,000. For an IRA, the limit is about $6,500. These limits can change each year.

As you begin to contribute to your retirement fund, it's wise to work on creating other sources of income.

Summary

1. 401k is a retirement fund where your employer puts away some money from your current salary into an investment account for when you retire.
2. The Traditional IRA is another type of retirement investment account where you do not pay taxes until you are ready to use the funds
3. The Roth IRA is a type of IRA where you pay taxes on your contributions now instead of later when you start to withdraw your money.
4. To take out the money from your 401k or IRA before retirement, you'll have to pay penalties
5. Don't only rely on your 401k. Have other stores of wealth.

www.ingramcontent.com/pod-product-compliance
Lightning Source LLC
Chambersburg PA
CBHW071122240526
45465CB00022B/780